B is for Bufflehead

by Steve Hutchcraft

PhotoHutch

www.photohutch.com

Contents

for
Heather
my little redhead

A is for

Auklet

Rhinoceros Auklet

I am a Rhinoceros Auklet, and I live on the ocean. Because I grow a big horn on top of my nose, I remind people of a rhinoceros. Though scientists have studied and studied my horn, no one knows why I have it, and I'm not telling!

a is for

avocet

American Avocet

American Avocets like me have very unique bills. Most shorebirds have thick bills for digging through yucky mud and sand. My bill is very thin and delicate. I gently sweep it through the water, feeling for tasty treats to eat.

B is for
Bufflehead

Bufflehead

People used to call me "Buffalo Head" because my big fluffy head looks too large for my little tiny body. Now, they just call me Bufflehead for short. Since I'm the smallest duck around, I've learned to catch and eat my food underwater to prevent bigger birds from stealing it.

b is for
booby

Blue-footed Booby

Blue-footed Boobies are the clowns of the bird world. Even our name comes from the Spanish word "bobo," meaning clown. Our men do a silly dance where they show off their beautiful blue feet. Scientists think it's to attract potential mates, but most of the time, it just makes us laugh.

9

C is for Caracara

Crested Caracara

I am a Crested Caracara. Though I look like an eagle, I'm actually a member of the falcon family. Unlike other falcons, I spend most of my time on the ground. With my long, powerful legs, I can walk and run with ease, dominating my competition at every feeding frenzy.

C is for
cuckoo

Yellow-billed Cuckoo

Yellow-billed Cuckoos don't live in clocks, and we don't eat Cocoa Puffs®. Instead, our favorite treats are hairy caterpillars. I like to roll them back and forth in my bill to loosen their hairs before I gobble 'em up. Later, I will spit all the icky hairs back out. Yummy, yummy in my tummy!

11

D is for
Dove

White-winged Dove   Mourning Dove

Doves like us eat lots and lots of hard seeds, so we swallow gravel and grit to help grind them up in our tummies. We need lots of water, too, and have learned a neat trick. Other birds have to tilt their heads back to drink. Not us, we can suck water straight into our bellies.

d is for

duck

Wood Duck

Wood Ducks look for cozy holes in tree trunks where we can build our nests. When I was only a day old, I leapt from my parents' nest to the ground where my mom was waiting to lead me to water. I was lucky! Some of my friends had to jump from nearly 300 feet high and walk over a mile.
What a tough first day they had!

E is for Eagle

Bald Eagle

I am a Bald Eagle. I am proud to be the national bird of the United States. My name is misleading because I'm not really bald. People just think that my beautiful head of white feathers makes me look that way.

14

Great Egrets are very graceful and elegant. Males like me perform beautiful displays to show off for the ladies. I spread my stunning feathers, point my bill to the sky, and stretch out my long neck again and again. It really drives them wild!

e is for
egret

Great Egret

F is for Flamingo

Greater Flamingo

Pink flamingos are found on lawns everywhere. However, real Greater Flamingos like me are a special treat to see. It's great fun to watch us eat. We stick our heads underwater, then squeeze lots of mud through our unusual bills, filtering out tasty morsels to eat.

16

Like our name suggests, flycatchers are great at catching flies. We even have whiskers that funnel bugs straight into our mouths. I am a Scissor-tailed Flycatcher, and my long tail opens and closes like scissors when I fly. My tail is so distinctive, you can identify me just from its shape.

f is for

flycatcher

Scissor-tailed Flycatcher

17

G is for Gull

Laughing Gull

When you are at the beach, do you hear somebody laughing? It's probably me, a Laughing Gull. My call sounds just like laughter. I'm not very good at catching food, but I am sneaky. My favorite trick is to land on a pelican's head and pluck food right out of its pouch.

18

g is for
grebe

Eared Grebe

Many birds change their appearance during the year, and I'm one of them. Each spring, my feathers change from boring dark grays and whites to beautiful deep oranges, reds, and blacks. To top it off, I grow gorgeous golden feathers on both sides of my head. That's why I'm called an Eared Grebe.

H is for
Heron

Great Blue
Heron

I am a Great Blue Heron, and I like to fish. Like all good fishermen, I am very patient. I will stand still in shallow water waiting for a fish to swim by. When I finally spot one, I will plunge my head into the water and catch it with my large, pointed bill.

20

h is for

hummingbird

Rufous Hummingbird

Hummingbirds are the flying jewels of the animal kingdom.
Not only are we beautiful, we are the only birds that can fly
forwards, backwards, sideways, and upside down. Our wings
beat so quickly that you can't even see them when we fly, but
you certainly can hear their hum!

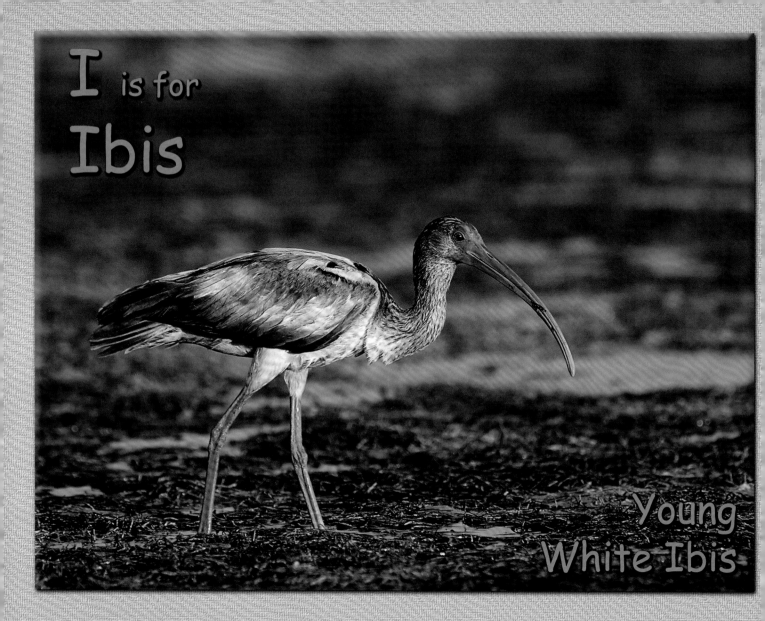

I is for
Ibis

Young
White Ibis

Young birds often look different from their parents. Like the baby swan in "The Ugly Duckling" fairy tale, young White Ibises aren't very pretty. We are brown and splotchy. Then, as we grow up, we transform into beautiful white birds with bright red legs and bright red beaks.

i is for

ibis

Adult
White Ibis

J is for
Jay

Green Jay

Jays are loud, lively, and smart. We work together in noisy flocks to look for food and to chase away large predators. Green Jays like me are really, really smart. I've even learned how to use sticks to dig bugs out of their hiding places.

Dark-eyed Juncos are a confusing bunch; we don't all look alike. In fact, there are seven types of us, each with a different color pattern. But, we all have white feathers in our tails that flash when we fly. We all love birdfeeders, too. One of us is probably at your feeder right now, but I bet it doesn't look like me!

25

j is for

junco

Dark-eyed Junco

K is for
Kite

White-tailed Kite

I am a White-tailed Kite. The kites you fly are actually named after my family. Like the toys, we are known for our easy, floating flight and swift swoops and dives. I am also one of the only large birds that can actually hover in place. This trick really me helps when I'm hunting for my food.

26

Many birds are named for the songs they sing. I sing "kis ka dee," and that's why people call me the Great Kiskadee. Unlike other songbirds, I like to dive into water. Sometimes, I'm after small fish to eat. More often, I dive in to clean my feathers. Taking a bath is really fun as I plunge into the water again and again and again.

k is for
kiskadee

Great Kiskadee

L is for
Loon

Common Loon

I am a Common Loon, and I am the national bird of Canada. Even though my picture is on the back of the Canadian Dollar, I may be better known for my haunting, yet beautiful cries that echo across the water. Danger lurks everywhere for our babies, so they often ride on our backs for protection.

Named for the little feathers on each side of my head, I am a Horned Lark. Just like a salmon, I return to my birthplace to nest and have my babies. Sometimes, I am so eager to get home and raise my family that I'll start building my nest well before spring has even sprung.

I is for **lark**

Horned Lark

M is for Meadowlark

Western Meadowlark

Not to be confused with my cousin, the Eastern Meadowlark, I am the Western Meadowlark. We may look a lot alike, but we are easy to tell apart because I am a much better singer. My joyful, flutelike song is so beautiful, it is often featured in movies.

Yellow-billed Magpies like me live only in California's Central and Coastal Valleys. Living in such a small area can be risky, and my family is in trouble. We have been hurt by disease and the loss of our oak woodland homes. We are depending on people like you to help us survive.

m is for
magpie

Yellow-billed Magpie

N is for **Night-Heron**

Yellow-crowned Night-Heron

I am a young Yellow-crowned Night-Heron. As my name suggests, I am more active at night. Sometimes, when I'm resting during the day, I'll stand facing the sun in a spread-wing pose. People haven't figured out why I do it, but I'll tell you what, it feels really good when I do.

32

Nuthatches are a lot of fun to watch. We dart along tree branches, hang upside down, and run straight down tree trunks. Staying warm at night is tough for us tiny Pygmy Nuthatches. Luckily, we are great snugglers, and as many as 100 of us will cuddle together to keep warm.

n is for nuthatch

Pygmy Nuthatch

O is for

Owl

Great Horned Owl

Owls are designed for hunting at night. We have large eyes and great hearing. Our feathers are very soft, allowing us to fly silently after our prey. A Great Horned Owl like me may look cute and fluffy, but I am actually one of the strongest and fiercest birds around.

O is for

oystercatcher

Like many birds, oystercatchers have bills designed for the foods we like to eat. I am a Black Oystercatcher, and I enjoy meals of mussels, clams, and of course, oysters. Luckily, my stout bill helps me open the hard shells so I can get to the tasty tidbits inside.

Black Oystercatcher

P is for

Pelican

Brown
Pelican

"A funny old bird is a pelican. His beak can hold more that his bellican. . ." I am a Brown Pelican. Unlike other pelicans, I dive into the water to catch fish with my huge beak. I'm a great flier, and it's fun to watch me catch waves like a surfer. Just inches off the water, I'll ride the air currents from wave after wave as I fly down the beach.

Horned Puffins are not very good fliers. We need to dive off cliffs or run along the water's surface to take flight. We are fast swimmers, though, and have specially designed beaks to help us catch and hold lots of little fish. In fact, someone once counted over 60 fish in my colorful beak.

p is for **puffin**

Horned Puffin

Q is for Quail

Scaled Quail

Quail live on the ground and often run away from danger instead of flying. Because we live in open, grassy areas that offer little protection, Scaled Quail have become the fastest runners of all quail. Even our babies are quick and can keep up with their parents when they are only one day old.

38

Northern Bobwhites like me are shy and secretive quail. My well-known "bob white" whistle is often the only sign that I'm around. Dust baths help me keep my feathers in tip-top shape and drive pesky bugs away. In this picture, I'm in a spin cycle, winding down my dust bath.

q is for quail

Northern Bobwhite

39

R is for Roadrunner

Greater Roadrunner

Greater Roadrunners don't go "beep beep" like the roadrunner in the cartoons. We are very fast, though, and I can run nearly 20 miles per hour. The desert where I live is hot during the day, but cold at night. Each morning, I turn my back towards the sun, fluff up my feathers, and soak in the sun's warmth.

It isn't very hard to guess why I'm called a Redhead. Some ducks dive underwater for their food. Others dabble, meaning they nibble at plants on the water's surface and tip over to pick at the plants below. I do both. And oddly, male Redheads like me don't quack; we meow and purr instead.

r is for
redhead

Redhead

41

S is for Spoonbill

Roseate Spoonbills have some of the neatest beaks in the bird world. They're shaped like giant spoons! We swing our bills through the water and snap them closed when we find food. Our pretty pink color comes from our food. The better we eat, the prettier and pinker we get!

Roseate Spoonbill

Though my name, Yellow-bellied Sapsucker, sounds like it came straight out of a cartoon, I really do exist. I'm one of the hardest working birds in the world. I tirelessly drill holes in tree trunks, creating a sap feast for me to enjoy. Lots of other birds and insects come by to feast on it, too.

43

S is for

sapsucker

Yellow-bellied Sapsucker

T is for

Titmouse

Tufted Titmouse

"Tit" is a British word meaning "little," and we do look like little mice as we scamper through the trees. Most Tufted Titmice have big topnotches of gray feathers. I am a Tufted Titmouse from Texas, and my tar-tinted topnotch is truly a treasure.

Terns are sleek and beautiful fliers. Unlike our rather ordinary cousins, the gulls, we have streamlined bodies with pointed wings, forked or notched tails, and sharp bills. While gulls scavenge, Royal Terns like me work hard for our food. We dive into the ocean from as high as 50 feet to catch our prey.

† is for

tern

Royal Tern

U is for Upland Sandpiper

Most sandpipers live along beaches and shorelines. I, an Upland Sandpiper, prefer prairies and meadows instead. I have very pretty wings that I like to show off. When I land, I always hold them up and pose so everyone can see their beauty.

Upland Sandpiper

V is for Verdin

Verdin

We Verdins are under-appreciated. In one bird book, we're even listed under "Drab Gray Birds of the Arid Southwest." With our yellow heads and bright red wing patches, I happen to think we are quite pretty. We are good nest builders, too, and we make separate homes for summer and winter use.

V is for
vulture

Turkey Vulture

Turkey Vultures are perfect for what we do: eat dead things. We use our great sense of smell to easily find stinky meals, even those hidden beneath a canopy of trees. Since we don't have feathers on our heads, we don't get all gooey when we eat yucky stuff. Disgusting, yes, but the world would be a lot smellier if we weren't around!

W is for Warbler

Worm-eating Warbler

Yellow Warbler

Red-faced Warbler

Black-throated Blue Warbler

Golden-cheeked Warbler

Black and White Warbler

Chestnut-sided Warbler

Yellow-rumped Warbler

We warblers are wonderful. We come in almost every color of the rainbow and have fun, descriptive names. I'm a Worm-eating Warbler, named after my favorite snack. My friends here are very unique, and their names describe how they look. Can you see why they have the names they do?

50

wren

Rock Wren

Marsh Wren

Cactus Wren

House Wren

Wrens are noisy defenders of our home territories. Our names often come from the places where we choose to live. Rock Wren likes rocky areas. Marsh Wren lives amongst the reeds. Cactus Wren prefers thorny bushes. I'm House Wren; can you guess where I like to live?

51

X is for Xantus's Murrelet

My name is pronounced "zan-toos mer-lit," and I am a difficult seabird to find. I spend most of my life way out at sea and only come to shore to nest with my mate. Soon after hatching, our babies climb out of the nest and jump into the ocean below. Then, as a family, we'll head back out to sea together.

Xantus's Murrelet

Y is for
Yellowlegs

Greater Yellowlegs

It's not hard to guess why I'm called a Greater Yellowlegs. In the fall and winter, I can be found living along many shorelines. But when I raise my family, I like privacy. So in the spring and summer, my family moves to a remote, mucky, mosquito-filled bog where nobody will bother us.

I am a Common Yellowthroat. Like most warblers, I migrate a long way between my summer and winter homes. Sometimes, I fly over hundreds of miles of water without stopping. When I finally reach land, I'm exhausted and need lots of food and rest before I can continue on my way.

Y is for

yellowthroat

Common
Yellowthroat

Z is for
Zone-tailed Hawk

Often, you can identify a hawk by the shape, size, and color of its tail. I'm a Zone-tailed Hawk, named for my tail of broad, black and white stripes. When I fly, I look a lot like a harmless Turkey Vulture. This resemblance really helps me sneak up on my unsuspecting prey. Hehehehe!

Zone-tailed
Hawk

It's a Who's Who Challenge . . . . .

I look pretty silly when I call, but my "hoos" can be heard from miles away.

(Great Horned Owl)

Though sometimes, I don't look like a bird at all, I really am a funny old bird whose beak can hold more than its belly can.

(Brown Pelican)

I'm just a big, harmless, bald-headed raptor. Try not to confuse me with a mean, tricky hawk that looks a lot like me.

(Turkey Vulture)

I look a lot like my dinosaur ancestors and can be found in many wetland areas.

(Great Blue Heron)

. . . . . who are these funny birds?

I can't forget to wash the back of my neck and behind my ears. . . .

(Dark-eyed Junco, Oregon race)

I'm not even fully grown, but I bet my tail already reminds you of something.

(Scissor-tailed Flycatcher)

Now that I'm an adult, it's easy to see that I was named for my fancy headdress.

(Yellow-crowned Night-Heron)

Do you remember that this is how I like to warm up on cold mornings?

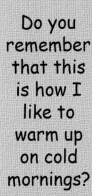

(Greater Roadrunner)

Who's Who Challenge . . . .

My dad does a silly dance, and when I grow up, I'll have very colorful feet.

(Blue-footed Booby)

Only able to chirp now, we will soon sing the song that gave us our name.

(Great Kiskadees)

I'll have to wait until I'm five before I get white feathers on my head and tail.

(Bald Eagle)

When we grow up, we'll be very elegant with long, beautiful white feathers.

(Great Egrets)

. . . . who are these babies?

We can't wait to learn to fish, but we'll need to learn patience first.

(Great Blue Herons)

I eat mostly seeds, and I can suck water straight into my belly.

(Mourning Dove)

Cute and cuddly now, we will grow up to be the fiercest birds around.

(Great Horned Owls)

Our beaks look just like something you eat with every day.

(Roseate Spoonbills)

More about the birds. . . .

A is for Auklet: *Rhinoceros Auklet*

Range:
Pacific Coast of North America.

Habitat:
Open ocean.

Food:
Fish and squid.

Fun Feathered Facts:
- Nests in burrows up to 20 feet long.
- Can dive to nearly 200 feet in search of food.
- Both the male and female grow a horn, though its function remains a mystery.

About the Photo:
A Rhinoceros Auklet in breeding plumage (bright, fancy feathers grown to attract a mate) a mile off the coast of Los Angeles, California.

a is for avocet: *American Avocet*

Range:
Western United States; occasional visitor to the East Coast.

Habitat:
Shallow, muddy, and marshy fresh and saltwater ponds and lakeshores.

Food:
Crustaceans, fish, and aquatic insects.

Fun Feathered Facts:
- To protect its delicate bill, it will use its feet and wings to drive away predators.
- Its alarm call gradually rises in pitch to sound as if it's approaching faster than it is.
- Only a day after hatching, chicks can walk, swim, and dive to escape danger.

About the Photo:
An American Avocet in breeding plumage; Kern National Wildlife Refuge, CA.

B is for Bufflehead: *Bufflehead*

Range:
Most of North America.

Habitat:
Summers on wooded lakes and ponds; winters on lakes and bays.

Food:
Insects, mollusks, and small fish.

Fun Feathered Facts:
- Smallest diving duck in North America.
- Nests in tree cavities and nest boxes.
- Returns with the same mate to the same nest for many years.

About the Photo:
A wintering Bufflehead on Morro Bay in California.

b is for booby: *Blue-footed Booby*

Range:
Rare visitor to the Southern California Coast and Salton Sea.

Habitat:
Lives on warm ocean waters and nests on rocky islands.

Food:
Fish, especially flying fish.

Fun Feathered Facts:
- Hunts in groups, but dines alone.
- An extremely streamlined body allows it to dive head first from as high as 80 feet.
- Male and female are nearly identical; female is "starry-eyed," with a star-shaped pupil.

About the Photo:
Courting Blue-footed Boobies at a colony in Banderas Bay in Mexico.

C is for Caracara: *Crested Caracara*

Range:
South Texas, Arizona, and Florida.
Habitat:
Dry scrub, deserts, and prairies.
Food:
Opportunistic scavenger; eats carrion (dead animals), small animals, insects, and even turtles.

Fun Feathered Facts:
- The name Caracara comes from its call.
- Regarded as the true national bird of Mexico.
- Betrays its regal appearance by flipping over cow patties in search of beetles.

About the Photo:
An adult Caracara at a watering hole in the Rio Grande Valley in Texas.

c is for cuckoo: *Yellow-billed Cuckoo*

Range:
Eastern U.S. to Colorado; rare to southeastern California.
Habitat:
Woods, forests, and thickets, especially those near water.
Food:
Insects, especially caterpillars.

Fun Feathered Facts:
- Very secretive; more often heard than seen.
- Remains still, waiting for prey to move, then makes crazy dashes to catch it.
- Egg laying is timed so hatching will coincide with peak caterpillar availability.

About the Photo:
A Yellow-billed Cuckoo in a mesquite thicket near water in the Rio Grande Valley in Texas.

D is for Dove: *White-winged Dove, Mourning Dove*

Range:
Mourning: most of North America.
White-winged: southwestern U.S. and Florida; expanding its range.
Habitat:
Mourning: everywhere.
White-winged: desert scrub.
Food:
Seeds, seeds, and more seeds.

Fun Feathered Facts:
- Powerful and swift fliers, doves can reach speeds of up to 55 miles per hour.
- Both mommy and daddy doves produce a nutritious fluid called "crop milk" that they feed to their babies.

About the Photo:
A White-winged Dove and a Mourning Dove at the Pond at Elephant Head near Tucson, Arizona.

d is for duck: *Wood Duck*

Range:
Northwestern and eastern United States; California.
Habitat:
Wooded ponds, lakes, and slow moving rivers and streams.
Food:
Mostly plants; occasionally insects, frogs, and small fish.

Fun Feathered Facts:
- The only dabbling duck that cavity nests.
- The female does all the courting, while the male plays hard to get.
- Because the ducklings leave the safety of the nest at such a small size, snapping turtles and large fish take a heavy toll on them.

About the Photo:
A Wood Duck drake (male) at Santee Lakes in San Diego County, CA.   63

E is for Eagle: *Bald Eagle*

Range:
Most of North America.

Habitat:
Usually near water.

Food:
Fish, ducks, and occasionally carrion.

Fun Feathered Facts:
- Can dive at over 100 miles per hour.
- Pairs build the largest nests of all birds; nests can weigh over 1,000 pounds and reach 12 feet tall.
- "Bald" is actually a shortened version of the word "Piebald," meaning "with patches of black and white."

About the Photo:
A wintering adult Bald Eagle in Homer, Alaska.

e is for egret: *Great Egret*

Range:
Temperate (not very cold) regions of the United States.

Habitat:
Wetlands.

Food:
Fish, reptiles, amphibians, and small mammals.

Fun Feathered Facts:
- Nests in rookeries (places in trees over water or on islands where groups of birds nest together).
- Egrets were almost hunted to extinction so their feathers could decorate women's hats. As a result, most birds are now protected by law.

About the Photo:
A male Great Egret during a courtship display at the Venice Rookery in Florida.

F is for Flamingo: *Greater Flamingo*

Range:
Casual visitor to the Gulf and southeastern Atlantic Coasts.

Habitat:
Shallow lagoons, ponds, and lakes; mudflats.

Food:
Shrimp, mollusks, and other tiny critters filtered out of mud.

Fun Feathered Facts:
- Its pink color comes from the food it eats.
- Nests in colonies and performs mass courtships where hundreds walk together in a parade.
- Because it eats with its head stuck in the mud underwater, it feeds in groups for protection.

About the Photo:
A Greater Flamingo in a freshwater pond on Pine Cay in the Turks and Caicos Islands.

f is for flycatcher: *Scissor-tailed Flycatcher*

Range:
South Central United States.

Habitat:
Open savannahs (grasslands scattered with trees).

Food:
Insects.

Fun Feathered Facts:
- Fiercely attacks hawks, owls, and crows that invade its nesting territory.
- Males perform beautiful courtship displays where they somersault and tumble in flight.
- Popular with farmers as it eats lots of crop-destroying insects.

About the Photo:
A Scissor-tailed Flycatcher, Rio Grande Valley, TX.

G is for Gull: *Laughing Gull*

Range:
Gulf and Atlantic Coasts, north to New England.

Habitat:
Ocean shorelines, harbors, estuaries, and parking lots.

Food:
Anything the waves wash up and whatever it can find or steal.

Fun Feathered Facts:
- The only gull that nests in the Southeastern United States.
- Social; feeds, travels, and rests in flocks.
- A very good flier; great at catching food tossed by beachgoers.

About the Photo:
A hungry flock of Laughing Gulls in nonbreeding plumage on Orange Beach in Alabama, eagerly awaiting bread tossed into the air by my wife.

g is for grebe: *Eared Grebe*

Range:
Central and western North America.

Habitat:
Winters on salt water; summers on lakes and in marshes.

Food:
Fish, crustaceans, mollusks, and aquatic insects.

Fun Feathered Facts:
- The most abundant grebe in the world.
- Over one million visit, feed, and nest on Mono Lake in California each year.
- Spends up to 10 months a year flightless as it prepares for migration, sometimes doubling its normal body weight in the process.

About the Photo:
An Eared Grebe in breeding plumage on Lake Merritt in Oakland, CA.

H is for Heron: *Great Blue Heron*

Range:
Most of North America.

Habitat:
Most freshwater habitats and coastal areas.

Food:
Anything it can catch: fish, birds, reptiles, amphibians, rodents, and insects.

Fun Feathered Facts:
- Nests in rookeries with other herons and egrets.
- Pairs have an elaborate nest building routine: the male flies in with a stick and presents it to his mate; she then works it into the nest.
- Not willing to give up a prize catch, it may choke to death on a fish too large to swallow.

About the Photo:
A nesting Great Blue Heron at the Venice Rookery, FL.

h is for hummingbird: *Rufous Hummingbird*

Range:
Western North America; occasionally visits the eastern U.S.

Habitat:
Meadows, gardens, and parks.

Food:
Nectar, sap, insects, and spiders.

Fun Feathered Facts:
- Weighs slightly more than a penny; eats up to eight times its body weight daily.
- Beats its wings up to 200 times per second and can reach speeds of 60 miles per hour.
- Relative to its size, its 3,900 mile migration is the longest in the bird world.

About the Photo:
A Rufous Hummingbird at the Pond at Elephant Head in Arizona.

I is for Ibis: _White Ibis_

Range:
Southeastern coastal states.
Habitat:
Saltwater and freshwater lakes and marshes; tidal flats.
Food:
Crabs, crawfish, insects, and frogs.

Fun Feathered Facts:
- Nests in huge colonies of up to 80,000 birds.
- Gathers together in large nighttime roosts.
- Lit by the setting sun, the long lines of ibises returning to the roost are a sight to see.

About the Photos:
Young White Ibis: Little Palm Island, FL.
Adult White Ibis: Six Mile Cypress Slough Preserve, FL.

J is for Jay: _Green Jay_

Range:
Lower Rio Grande Valley, Texas.
Habitat:
Mesquite scrub and riparian (streamside) woodlands.
Food:
Insects, nuts, berries, and seeds.

Fun Feathered Facts:
- Very smart with a great memory; it can remember where it stored food months before.
- Families stay together; the one-year-olds help their parents protect the new babies.

About the Photo:
A Green Jay at the Martin Javelina Refuge near McAllen, Texas.

j is for junco: _Dark-eyed Junco_

Range:
Most of North America.
Habitat:
Prefers wooded habitats, especially coniferous (cone bearing) woods.
Food:
Seeds.

Fun Feathered Facts:
- Feeds on the ground, especially beneath feeders, feasting on the seed spilled by other birds.
- Seven distinct variations include: Oregon (shown here), Pink-sided, White-winged, Slate-colored, Gray-headed, Red-backed, and the critically endangered Guadalupe.

About the Photo:
A Dark-eyed Junco in an artificial stream in Alamo, CA.

K is for Kite: _White-tailed Kite_

Range:
Pacific Coast states, Texas coastal areas, and South Florida.
Habitat:
Grasslands with scattered trees.
Food:
Mostly rodents.

Fun Feathered Facts:
- Hunts by hovering above, then dropping down onto prey.
- Forms winter roosts of over 100 birds.
- Once known as the Black-shouldered Kite. Can you see why?

About the Photo:
A White-tailed Kite perched along a highway near the Aransas National Wildlife Refuge in Texas.

k is for kiskadee: *Great Kiskadee*

Range:
South Texas; visits southwest Louisiana and southeast Arizona.

Habitat:
Dense woods and thickets, usually near water.

Food:
Insects, lizards, berries, and occasionally fish.

Fun Feathered Facts:
- Hunts from a perch; will dive onto prey, then fly back up to dine.
- The first bird to begin singing each morning.
- Fears the coral snake and avoids anything with the same colors: red, black, and yellow.

About the Photo:
A Great Kiskadee at a watering hole on the Martin Javelina Refuge near McAllen, Texas.

L is for Loon: *Common Loon*

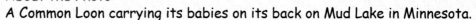

Range:
Winters on both coasts; summers in the northern United States and Canada.

Habitat:
Winters on salt water; summers on freshwater lakes and large ponds.

Food:
Fish.

Fun Feathered Facts:
- With its feet near its tail, it's a great swimmer, but awkward, even "loonie," on land.
- Can dive 200 feet below the surface and can stay underwater for up to 3 minutes.
- Has sharp points on the roof of its mouth and tongue to help it hold onto slippery fish.

About the Photo:
A Common Loon carrying its babies on its back on Mud Lake in Minnesota.

l is for lark: *Horned Lark*

Range:
All of North America, except the Gulf Coast and Florida.

Habitat:
Open country, especially barren ground with scattered bushes.

Food:
Adults eat seeds; young are fed insects and spiders.

Fun Feathered Facts:
- The only true lark in North America.
- Walks and runs on the ground when feeding; doesn't hop like most birds.
- During courtship, males impress females by raising their "horns" and flying 800 feet high while singing.

About the Photo:
A Horned Lark getting a drink at the Silver Saddle Ranch in the high desert of California.

M is for Meadowlark: *Western Meadowlark*

Range:
Western North America; occasionally visits the East Coast.

Habitat:
Open grasslands.

Food:
Insects and seeds.

Fun Feathered Facts:
- Nests on the ground; unfortunately, the mowing of fields destroys many nests.
- Nests are often covered by roofs of grass and have entrance tunnels several feet long.
- Frequently seen singing on roadside fence posts.

About the Photo:
A Western Meadowlark proudly singing while perched alongside a quiet road in Byron, California.

m is for magpie: *Yellow-billed Magpie*

Range:
California's Central and Coastal Valleys.

Habitat:
Open oak woodlands.

Food:
Pretty much anything it can find.

Fun Feathered Facts:
- Feeds on the ground.
- Builds large, domed nests up to 3 feet across.
- West Nile Virus (spread by mosquitoes) and habitat destruction have decreased its population by more than 50% over the last few years.

About the Photo:
A Yellow-billed Magpie at the Del Valle Regional Park in Livermore, California.

N is for Night-Heron: *Yellow-crowned Night-Heron*

Range:
East Coast and central United States.

Habitat:
Shallow ponds and marshes.

Food:
Crabs and crawfish.

Fun Feathered Facts:
- Nocturnal, meaning it hunts for food at night and rests during the day.
- Waits patiently for prey to come near or slowly walks in search of it.

About the Photo:
A juvenile Yellow-crowned Night-Heron at the Six Mile Cypress Slough Preserve in Florida.

n is for nuthatch: *Pygmy Nuthatch*

Range:
Western United States.

Habitat:
Coniferous forests, especially those with Ponderosa Pines.

Food:
Insects and seeds.

Fun Feathered Facts:
- One of the only songbirds that has helpers at the nest; one-year-olds typically help their parents with the new babies.
- Employs 3 tactics to survive cold nights: roosting together, roosting in tree cavities, and safely dropping its body temperature (called torpor).

About the Photo:
A Pygmy Nuthatch in the Kaibab National Forest, AZ.

O is for Owl: *Great Horned Owl*

Range:
All of North America, except the extreme north.

Habitat:
Mainly woods and forests.

Food:
Mammals and birds.

Fun Feathered Facts:
- Female is larger; male's voice is deeper.
- Often swallows prey whole, later regurgitating pellets of fur, bones, and other undigested stuff.
- The only animal to regularly dine on skunk.
- Can rotate its head three quarters of the way around on its neck.

About the Photo:
A Great Horned Owl near our deck in Alamo, CA.

o is for oystercatcher: *Black Oystercatcher*

Range:
West Coast, north to Alaska.
Habitat:
Rocky shorelines and occasionally, tidal flats.
Food:
Mussels, limpets, clams, and oysters.

Fun Feathered Facts:
- Feeds at low tide, when mollusks are exposed; rests at high tide.
- Nests on rocky islands.
- Parents care for their young for a longer time than other shorebird parents care for theirs.

About the Photo:
A Black Oystercatcher patrolling a tidal flat at the Albany Bulb in California.

P is for Pelican: *Brown Pelican*

Range:
West, Gulf, and Southeast Coasts.
Habitat:
Ocean shores and bays.
Food:
Fish.

Fun Feathered Facts:
- The Pacific sub-species boasts a more colorful breeding plumage than its eastern cousin.
- Warms its eggs with its feet, not with its breast feathers like most birds do.
- Performs strange looking head throws where it stretches its pouch back over its head.

About the Photo:
A Brown Pelican showing its pouch in La Jolla, CA.

p is for puffin: *Horned Puffin*

Range:
Northern Pacific Coast.
Habitat:
Open ocean; nests on rocky cliffs.
Food:
Fish and squid.

Fun Feathered Facts:
- Nests in rock crevices and short burrows.
- Is deceptively colored to fool predators. When seen from above, its dark back blends in with the water's surface. When seen from below, its white belly blends in with the sky.

About the Photo:
A Horned Puffin in a rock crevice above the Prince William Sound in Alaska.

Q is for Quail: *Scaled Quail*

Range:
Parts of Arizona, Colorado, Kansas, New Mexico, Oklahoma, and Texas.
Habitat:
Arid, brushy grassland.
Food:
Seeds, beetles, and grasshoppers.

Fun Feathered Facts:
- Named for the scale-like feathers on its breast.
- Females will lay as many as 14 eggs.
- Chicks grow so quickly that they are the size of adults within 12 weeks and have their own babies within a year.

About the Photo:
A Scaled Quail atop a Black Bush Acacia at the Seminole Canyon State Park in Texas.

q is for quail: _Northern Bobwhite_

Range:
Central and eastern United States; eastern Washington.

Habitat:
Brushy grasslands and woodlands.

Food:
Seeds, leaves, berries, and insects.

Fun Feathered Facts:
- Finding safety in numbers, quail form groups, called coveys, of up to 30 birds.
- Hunting and loss of suitable habitat have caused its population to decline significantly, and in some areas, to disappear completely.

About the Photo:
A Northern Bobwhite finishing a dust bath in the Rio Grande Valley in Texas.

R is for Roadrunner: _Greater Roadrunner_

Range:
Southwestern United States.

Habitat:
Open deserts and arid grasslands.

Food:
Anything it can catch.

Fun Feathered Facts:
- Eats many venomous animals like rattlesnakes, scorpions, and spiders.
- Often jumps into the air to catch low-flying birds.

About the Photo:
A close-up of a Greater Roadrunner near a watering hole in the Rio Grande Valley in Texas.

r is for redhead: _Redhead_

Range:
Most of North America.

Habitat:
Winters on large bays and lakes; summers on marshy lakes and ponds.

Food:
Water plants, insects, and mollusks.

Fun Feathered Facts:
- Feeds early and late in the day, sometimes even at night.
- Though it does raise some of its own babies, it will also lay eggs in the nests of other birds. When those babies hatch, the other birds will raise them as their own.

About the Photo:
A Redhead drake on San Diego Bay in California.

S is for Spoonbill: _Roseate Spoonbill_

Range:
Gulf Coast.

Habitat:
Mangrove swamps, tidal ponds, and saltwater lagoons.

Food:
Mollusks, small fish, and aquatic insects.

Fun Feathered Facts:
- "Roseate" refers to its pink color.
- Nests in rookeries with herons and egrets.
- Like egrets, spoonbills were hunted to the brink of extinction for their feathers.

About the Photo:
A Roseate Spoonbill atop a snag at the Smith Oaks Bird Sanctuary in High Island, Texas.

s is for sapsucker: *Yellow-bellied Sapsucker*

Range:
Eastern United States through much of Canada.
Habitat:
Woodlands and orchards.
Food:
Sap and bugs stuck in sap.

Fun Feathered Facts:
- Makes two types of holes: deep round ones and shallower, rectangular ones.
- Its saliva prevents the holes from plugging up.
- Drums with its bill to define its territory, and often beats on metal signs and manmade objects to make its drumming louder.

About the Photo:
A Yellow-bellied Sapsucker in Huntsville, Alabama.

T is for Titmouse: *Tufted Titmouse*

Range:
Eastern United States, south through Texas.
Habitat:
Woodlands and forests.
Food:
Seeds, berries, and insects.

Fun Feathered Facts:
- Spends its entire life very close to its birthplace.
- Thinner birds are more dominant than fatter ones and are higher in titmouse social status.
- The Black-crested Tufted Titmouse (shown) is only found in Texas.

About the Photo:
A Black-crested Tufted Titmouse in the Rio Grande Valley in Texas.

t is for tern: *Royal Tern*

Range:
East, Gulf, and Southern California coasts.
Habitat:
Shorelines, estuaries, and bays.
Food:
Fish.

Fun Feathered Facts:
- Makes its nest in a scrape on a low-lying island.
- Babies leave the nest a day after hatching and gather in a large group of thousands of chicks.
- Parents feed only their own chicks, and amazingly, they are able to find them in the crowd.

About the Photo:
A Royal Tern having a bad hair day in La Jolla, CA.

U is for Upland Sandpiper: *Upland Sandpiper*

Range:
Eastern and central North America.
Habitat:
Prairies and meadows.
Food:
Worms, grasshoppers, and other insects.

Fun Feathered Facts:
- Loss of habitat has caused a significant decline in the population of this once common bird.
- With so little appropriate habitat in the Northeast, it nests around and in between airport runways.

About the Photos:
Upland Sandpipers posing on rocks on the Felton Prairie in Minnesota.

71

V is for Verdin: *Verdin*

Range:
Desert Southwest.

Habitat:
Desert scrub, especially with thorny bushes.

Food:
Insects, seeds, and berries.

Fun Feathered Facts:
- Builds nests all year long. Summer nests are well ventilated to help keep cool; winter nests are well insulated to help stay warm.
- Builds nests for roosting, too, that are smaller than those built for raising babies.

About the Photo:
A beautiful Verdin at a pond in the Rio Grande Valley in Texas.

v is for vulture: *Turkey Vulture*

Range:
Most of North America.

Habitat:
All habitats, but prefers open country.

Food:
Carrion.

Fun Feathered Facts:
- Named for its similarity to the Wild Turkey.
- Flies with its wings in a "V," allowing it to fly very close to the ground and tree tops to help it pick up the scent of a potential meal.

About the Photo:
A Turkey Vulture on a dry lake bed at the Kern National Wildlife Refuge in California.

W is for Warbler: *Worm-eating Warbler*

Range:
Eastern United States.

Habitat:
Dense shrubs, often on steep slopes.

Food:
Caterpillars, spiders, and slugs.

Fun Feathered Facts:
- If a predator approaches when her eggs are ready to hatch, the mother will remain still and leave her eggs only if she's touched.

About the Photo:
A Worm-eating Warbler in the Appalachians.

W is for Warbler: *Yellow Warbler*

Range:
North America.

Habitat:
Brushy areas and wet thickets.

Food:
Insects.

Fun Feathered Facts:
- Has the widest range of all North American warblers.

About the Photo:
A Yellow Warbler in the Rio Grande Valley in Texas.

W is for Warbler: *Red-faced Warbler*

Range:
Arizona and New Mexico mountains.

Habitat:
Mountain canyons.

Food:
Insects and small fruits.

Fun Feathered Facts:
- Very sensitive to habitat disturbances, it will vanish from an area if there's too much human activity.

About the Photo:
A Red-faced Warbler, Gila National Forest, NM.

W is for Warbler: _Black-throated Blue Warbler_

Range:
Eastern North America.
Habitat:
Shrubs and thickets in forests.
Food:
Insects and small fruits.

Fun Feathered Facts:
👓 Males and females look so unalike, they were once thought to be different species.
About the Photo:
A Black-throated Blue Warbler on Little Palm Island in the Florida Keys.

W is for Warbler: _Golden-cheeked Warbler_

Range:
Hill Country of Texas.
Habitat:
Ashe Juniper Woodlands.
Food:
Insects.

Fun Feathered Facts:
👓 Critically endangered due to habitat loss in its small breeding and wintering ranges.
About the Photo:
A Golden-cheeked Warbler on a juniper at the Pedernales Falls State Park in Texas.

W is for Warbler: _Black and White Warbler_

Range:
East Coast to the Rocky Mountains.
Habitat:
Woodlands, preferably damp ones.
Food:
Caterpillars, insects, and spiders.

Fun Feathered Facts:
👓 Has an extra long hind toe and claw to help hold onto tree trunks and branches.
About the Photo:
A Black and White Warbler near the Blue Ridge Parkway in North Carolina.

W is for Warbler: _Chestnut-sided Warbler_

Range:
East Coast through the Great Plains.
Habitat:
Thickets and undergrowth in woods.
Food:
Insects.

Fun Feathered Facts:
👓 Sings two songs: an accented "pleased to MEET YA" song to attract mates and an unaccented version used to defend territory.
About the Photo:
A Chestnut-sided Warbler in the Appalachians.

W is for Warbler: _Yellow-rumped Warbler_

Range:
Most of North America.
Habitat:
Open woods.
Food:
Insects and berries.

Fun Feathered Facts:
👓 The ability to digest the waxy fruit of wax myrtle and bayberry plants allows it to winter farther north than other warblers.
About the Photo:
A Yellow-rumped Warbler in Alamo, California.

w is for wren: _Rock Wren_

Range:
Western United States.
Habitat:
Rocky areas.
Food:
Insects and spiders.

Fun Feathered Facts:
👓 Sings over 100 different songs.
👓 Paves a path to its nest with pebbles.
About the Photo:
A Rock Wren on the cliffs of La Jolla, California.

73

w is for wren: *Marsh Wren*

Range:
Most of North America.
Habitat:
Marshes, especially with cattails.
Food:
Aquatic insects and spiders.

Fun Feathered Facts:
👀 Western and eastern birds look a little different and sing very different songs. They may, in fact, be two species.
About the Photo:
A Marsh Wren at the Anahuac N.W.R. in Texas.

w is for wren: *Cactus Wren*

Range:
Desert Southwest.
Habitat:
Deserts with cacti.
Food:
Insects, spiders, and berries.

Fun Feathered Facts:
👀 Builds a large, football-shaped nest tucked into a cactus or thorny bush.
About the Photo:
A Cactus Wren in the Sonoran Desert in Arizona.

w is for wren: *House Wren*

Range:
Much of North America.
Habitat:
Woods and suburbs.
Food:
Insects and spiders.

Fun Feathered Facts:
👀 A male may put as many as 400 sticks into a nest cavity, where his mate will complete the nest and add its soft lining of grasses.
About the Photo:
A House Wren near Lake Owassa in New Jersey.

X is for Xantus's: *Xantus's Murrelet*

Range:
Southern Pacific coast of North America.
Habitat:
Open ocean; nests on only a few islands off Southern and Baja California.
Food:
Fish and squid.

Fun Feathered Facts:
👀 Probably the rarest of all seabirds with a population of only 10,000.
👀 Almost always feeds in pairs, even during nesting season when its mate is on the nest.
👀 Nests in a crevice or burrow; only approaches its nest after dusk and leaves before dawn.
About the Photos:
A pair of Xantus's Murrelets feeding in the Santa Monica Bay, CA.

Y is for Yellowlegs: *Greater Yellowlegs*

Range:
Most of North America.
Habitat:
Winters along shorelines; summers in bogs and swamps.
Food:
In winter, eats mollusks, small fish, and aquatic animals; in summer, eats primarily insects.

Fun Feathered Facts:
👀 Very noisy; often announces its arrival with an ear-piercing call.
👀 Chases down fast-moving prey in the shallows.
👀 Also feeds by swinging its bill from side to side, stirring up tasty tidbits to eat.
About the Photo:
A Greater Yellowlegs patrolling the shoreline of a tidal flat at the Hayward Interpretive Center in California.

y is for yellowthroat: *Common Yellowthroat*

Range:
Most of North America.
Habitat:
Wet thickets and wetlands.
Food:
Insects and spiders.

Fun Feathered Facts:
- Males flutter into the air to attract mates.
- Females seem to prefer males with larger masks.
- Nests are well hidden, typically in thick shrubs; to help keep their locations secret, parents will approach and leave them using different routes.

About the Photo:
A singing Common Yellowthroat at the Stone Mountain Park in Georgia.

Z is for Zone-tailed Hawk: *Zone-tailed Hawk*

Range:
Extreme southwestern United States.
Habitat:
Canyons and riparian woods.
Food:
Small mammals and birds.

Fun Feathered Facts:
- Participates in spectacular aerial courtships where the male and female perform loops, rolls, and dives together.
- Aggressively defends its nesting area, chasing much larger animals, including humans, away.

About the Photos:
Zone-tailed Hawks in flight and perched at the Boyce Thompson Arboretum in Arizona.

Contents Page: *Painted Bunting*

Range:
South central and southeastern coastal United States.
Habitat:
Brushy areas and thickets.
Food:
Seeds and insects.

Fun Feathered Facts:
- Males are highly territorial and may even fight to the death over a prime spot.
- Populations are declining significantly due to habitat loss and the pet trade industry. Each year, thousands of brightly colored males are trapped in Mexico and sold to European caged-bird dealers.

About the Photo:
A male Painted Bunting in the Rio Grande Valley, TX.

Dedication Page: *Red-headed Woodpecker*

Range:
Central and eastern United States; southeastern Canada.
Habitat:
Open woodlands.
Food:
Acorns, beechnuts, and other nuts; insects, fruits, and berries.

Fun Feathered Facts:
- The most omnivorous (meaning it will eat lots of different things) woodpecker in North America.
- Often catches insects in midair.
- Caches (stores) food in tree cracks and covers it with slivers of wood to hide it from other birds.

About the Photo:
A Red-headed Woodpecker at Okatibbee Lake in Mississippi.

75

Resources Page: *Short-eared Owl*

Range:
Most of North America; Hawaii too!

Habitat:
Open grasslands, tundra, and marshes.

Food:
Small mammals and birds.

Fun Feathered Facts:
- Named for the small tufts of feathers on its head.
- Flies more than most owls; with its deep wingbeats, it looks like a giant moth when flying.
- Unlike nocturnal owls, it hunts at dawn and dusk, flying back and forth over fields and marshes in search of prey.

About the Photo:
A Short-eared Owl in flight in Byron, California.

About the Book Page: *Northern Harrier*

Range:
Most of North America.

Habitat:
Open fields and prairies, particularly those near water.

Food:
Rodents, amphibians, reptiles, and birds.

Fun Feathered Facts:
- Also known as a Marsh Hawk, it is often seen flying low over fields and marshes.
- Unlike other hawks, it uses its sense of hearing to help it find prey.
- Males mate with as many as five females and will bring food to each mate and her nest of babies.

About the Photo:
A diving Northern Harrier in Byron, California.

Acknowledgements Page: *Grasshopper Sparrow*

Range:
Eastern North America, the Great Plains, and California.

Habitat:
Prairies and dry grasslands.

Food:
Insects, including of course, grasshoppers, and seeds.

Fun Feathered Facts:
- Not only does it love to eat grasshoppers, it sings like one, too.
- A Grasshopper Sparrow will pull off all the legs of a grasshopper before eating it or feeding it to nestlings.

About the Photo:
A singing Grasshopper Sparrow on a thistle in the Bishop Ranch Regional Preserve in San Ramon, CA.

Copyright Page: *Common Moorhen*

Range:
Eastern and southwestern United States; southern Canada.

Habitat:
Freshwater marshes and ponds.

Food:
Seeds, plants, insects, and snails.

Fun Feathered Facts:
- Also known as a Red-billed Mudhen.
- Extra long toes help it walk on floating plants.
- Babies are born with spurs on their wings to help them climb around on vegetation.

About the Photo:
A Common Moorhen screaming at an American Alligator in Lake Martin in Louisiana.

Birds are amazing creatures, and I learned more about them than I ever imagined while researching this book. Even more amazing is the wealth of information available in print and on the web. The following is a list of resources I used gathering information for this book. I recommend them for further education and enjoyment.

Print

Field Guide to the Birds of North America. Washington, D.C. : National Geographic, 1999.

Reference Atlas to the Birds of North America. Washington, D.C. : National Geographic, 2003.

Sibley, David Allen. *The Sibley Guide to Birds.* New York: Alfred A Knopf, 2000.

Stokes, Donald & Lillian. *Stokes Field Guide to Birds, Western Region.* Boston: Little, Brown and Company, 1996.

Stokes, Donald & Lillian. *Stokes Field Guide to Birds, Eastern Region.* Boston: Little, Brown and Company, 1996.

Eaton, Joe. "Wild Neighbors: West Nile Virus Hits the Yellow-billed Magpie," *The Berkeley Daily Planet,* October 9, 2008.

Shalaway, Scott. "Wildlife: How to Help Birds Beat the Heat," *Pittsburgh Post-Gazette,* June 26, 2005.

Anderson, Hans Christian. "The Ugly Duckling." 1843.

Merritt, Dixon Lanier. "A Funny Old Bird is a Pelican." 1910.

Web

All About Birds. Cornell Lab of Ornithology.
www.allaboutbirds.org

All-Birds.com.
www.all-birds.com

The Birds of North America Online. Cornell Lab of Ornithology.
bna.birds.cornell.edu/bna

Birds of Oklahoma. Bill Horn.
www.birdsofoklahoma.net

BirdWeb. Seattle Audubon Society.
www.birdweb.org

Chipper Woods Bird Observatory. Indianapolis, IN.
www.wbu.com/chipperwoods

Creagrus @ Monterey Bay. Don Roberson.
creagrus.home.montereybay.com

eNature.
www.enature.com

The Firefly Forest. T. Beth Kinsey.
www.fireflyforest.net/firefly

Hinterland Who's Who. Canadian Wildlife Service, Canadian Wildlife Federation.
www.hww.ca

Honolulu Zoo.
www.honoluluzoo.org

National Audubon Society.
www.audubon.org/bird

National Geographic.
animals.nationalgeographic.com/animals/birds

NatureWorks. New Hampshire Public Television.
www.nhptv.org/natureworks

Outdoor Alabama. Alabama Department of Conservation and Natural Resources.
www.outdooralabama.com/outdoor-alabama

Patuxent Bird Identification InfoCenter. United States Geological Survey
www.mbr-pwrc.usgs.gov

The Peregrine Fund.
www.peregrinefund.org

Peterson Field Guides.
www.houghtonmifflinbooks.com/peterson/resources/identifications

The Smithsonian Institution.
www.si.edu

Arizona-Sonora Desert Museum.
www.desertmuseum.org

Stanford Birds.
www.stanford.edu/group/stanfordbirds

Stokes Birds at Home.
www.stokesbirdsathome.com

Texas Parks and Wildlife.
www.tpwd.state.tx.us

The Raptor Center, University of Minnesota.
www.raptor.cvm.umn.edu

The Virtual Nature Trail at Penn State, New Kensington.
www.psu.edu/dept/nkbiology/naturetrail

whatBird.com. Mitch Waite Group.
www.whatbird.com

World of Hummingbirds.
www.worldofhummingbirds.com

Wildlifedepartment.com. Oklahoma Department of Wildlife Conservation.
www.wildlifedepartment.com

Wild Ones Animal Index. Wildlife Trust.
www.thewildones.org

Trademarks

"Cocoa Puffs®," General Mills, Inc., Minneapolis, MN.

About the Book

When I was looking for a way to use my photography to help introduce my daughter to the wonders of nature, a friend suggested creating an ABC photo book. My first thought was "aren't there enough of those already?"

After some thought and a little research, my wife and I decided to create an ABC book that would introduce kids to the birds of North America. We wanted to engage little ones without intimidating them, so choosing the right birds to include was essential.

We started with a target list of silly sounding names and funny looking birds. We then added birds that had interesting stories to tell. We had no choice for the letters U, X, and Z, as only one species occurs in North America for each of them. Finally, after two years of chasing birds around the country, I completed the photography.

The showcased birds have a mix of fun names, fascinating personalities, and unique behaviors. The book's layout is designed to be easily adapted to each child's level. The photos, letters, and names are perfect for the earliest learners. The accompanying text is intended to intrigue young children with a few fun facts about each bird. For older kids (and adults), I've provided a section that offers more detailed information on each species, including range, habitat, and feeding preferences. For fun, I've also included a section of baby birds and interesting images for a who's who challenge.

Throughout the process of creating this book, my knowledge and appreciation of birds has grown tremendously. I've also succeeded in exposing our little one to their marvels. I'll never forget the experience of trying to photograph with her sitting on my lap, squealing with delight as each new bird approached. Hopefully, her enjoyment of our feathered friends will last a lifetime.

I hope you enjoy the book and that you, too, will find a love and appreciation for the birds that inspired it.

Acknowledgements

I am truly indebted to the many people who have helped and encouraged me throughout this project. First and foremost is my wife, June, for her advice and editing, support and encouragement, patience and love. My daughter, Heather, for her candid likes and dislikes of the photos and abject disinterest in an early text. My mom for her advice and support, sister Pam, niece Kate, and nephew Peter for their opinions on the photographs and text. Also, thanks to Nichole Pera, Ted Robertson, Patti Harris, John Schaust, and my mother-in-law Mary Ann Thigpen for editorial help and to Cecil Williams for her enthusiastic support of the project.

Locating the birds I needed to complete the alphabet was simplified by the birding listservs on the internet. The people on Minnesota's "mnbird" listserv helped me track down the Upland Sandpiper. In particular, I would like to thank Randy Frederickson who volunteered to be my loon guide for a day. The folks on Arizona and New Mexico's "BIRDWG05" listserv pointed me to potential spots for Zone-tailed Hawks. The people on Mt. Diablo Audubon's "EBB Sightings" listserv patiently helped me find targeted birds in my own area. Subscribe to a listserv in your area; you never know what you might find.

The most trying bird in my quest was by far the Xantus's Murrelet. After several failed attempts to find one, I successfully turned to the Los Angeles Audubon Society. Each year, they organize several wonderful pelagic trips led by amazing guides.

And finally, I want to thank my father, who instilled in me a love for birds and nature that has lasted me a lifetime. I hope he's proud of this accomplishment.

—Steve